Behind or In Front Of

by Wiley Blevins

raintree

a Capstone company—publishers for children

www.raintree.co.uk

Raintree is an imprint of Capstone Global Library Limited, a company incorporated in England and Wales having its registered office at 264 Banbury Road, Oxford, OX2 7DY – Registered company number: 6695582

www.raintree.co.uk
myorders@raintree.co.uk

Edited by Erika Shores
Designed by Elyse White
Picture research by Tracy Cummins
Production by Laura Manthe
Originated by Capstone Global Library Limited
Printed and bound in India

ISBN 978 1 4747 6874 0 (hardback)
ISBN 978 1 4747 6889 4 (paperback)

British Library Cataloguing in Publication Data
A full catalogue record for this book is available from the British Library.

Acknowledgements
iStockphoto: Shooki; Shutterstock: Enrichetta de Simon, 5, Hannamaria MommaAbbott, Design Element, Noskov Vladimir, Cover Left, photolinc, Design Element, robert cicchetti, 19, Roschetzky Photography, 21, Shannon Jordan, 11, shutterupeire, 17, Snowflizz, 7, Teri Virbickis, 9.

Every effort has been made to contact copyright holders of material reproduced in this book. Any omissions will be rectified in subsequent printings if notice is given to the publisher.

Contents

Where is it?

Look around!

Can you see the cat?

The cat is behind the door.

Meeow!

In the country

The fence is in front of
the horses. The horses
are behind the fence.
How many horses can
you see?

The pond is in front of
the barn.

What colour is the barn?

The ducklings swim behind their mother. The mother swims in front of the ducklings. Quack! Quack! Quack!

The pumpkins are in front of the sign. The sign is behind the pumpkins. How many pumpkins can you see?

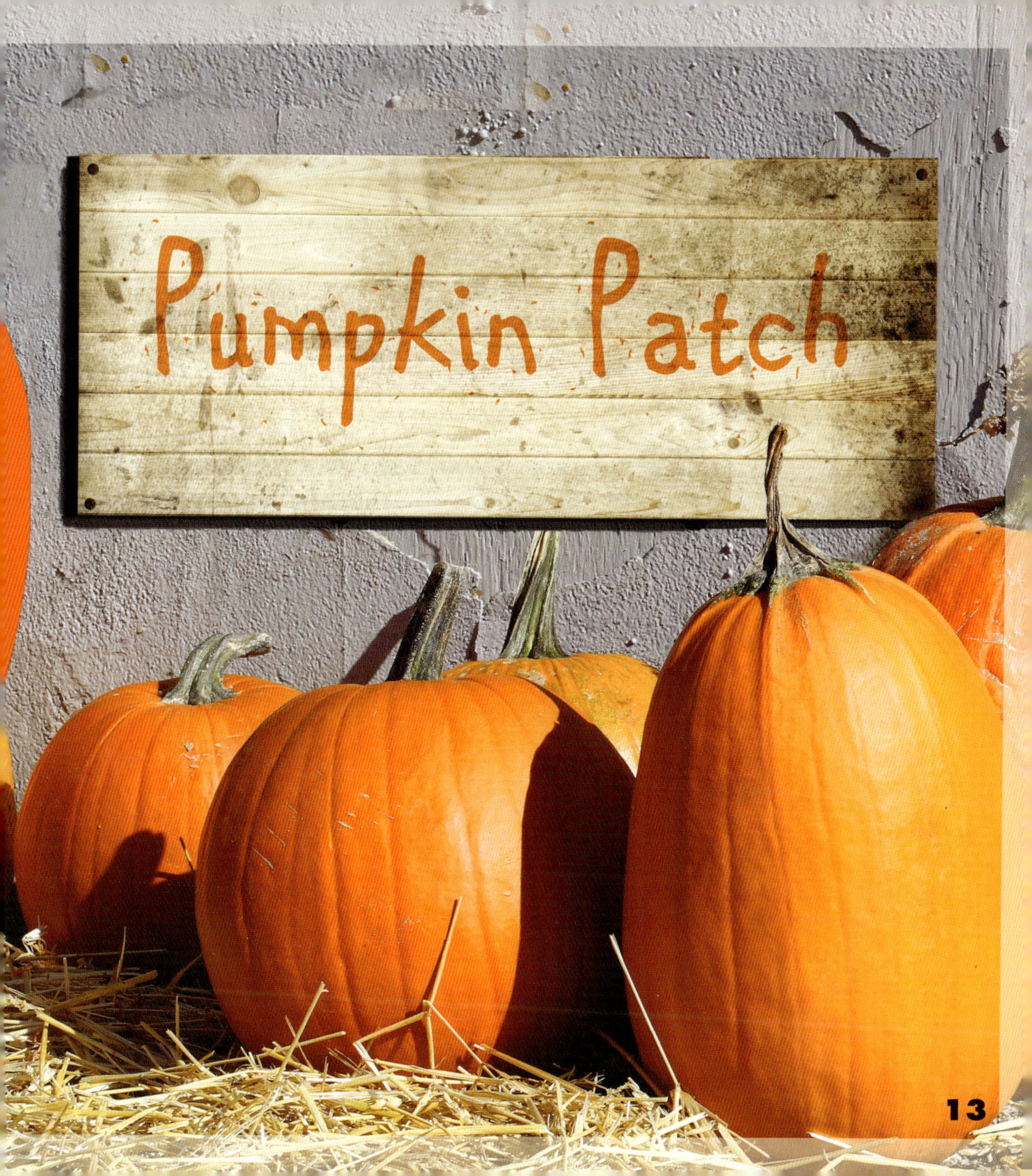
Pumpkin Patch

The dog is behind
the fence. The fence
keeps the dog in.
What colour is the dog?

In the city

This is the Statue of Liberty.
The statue is in front of
the city of New York.

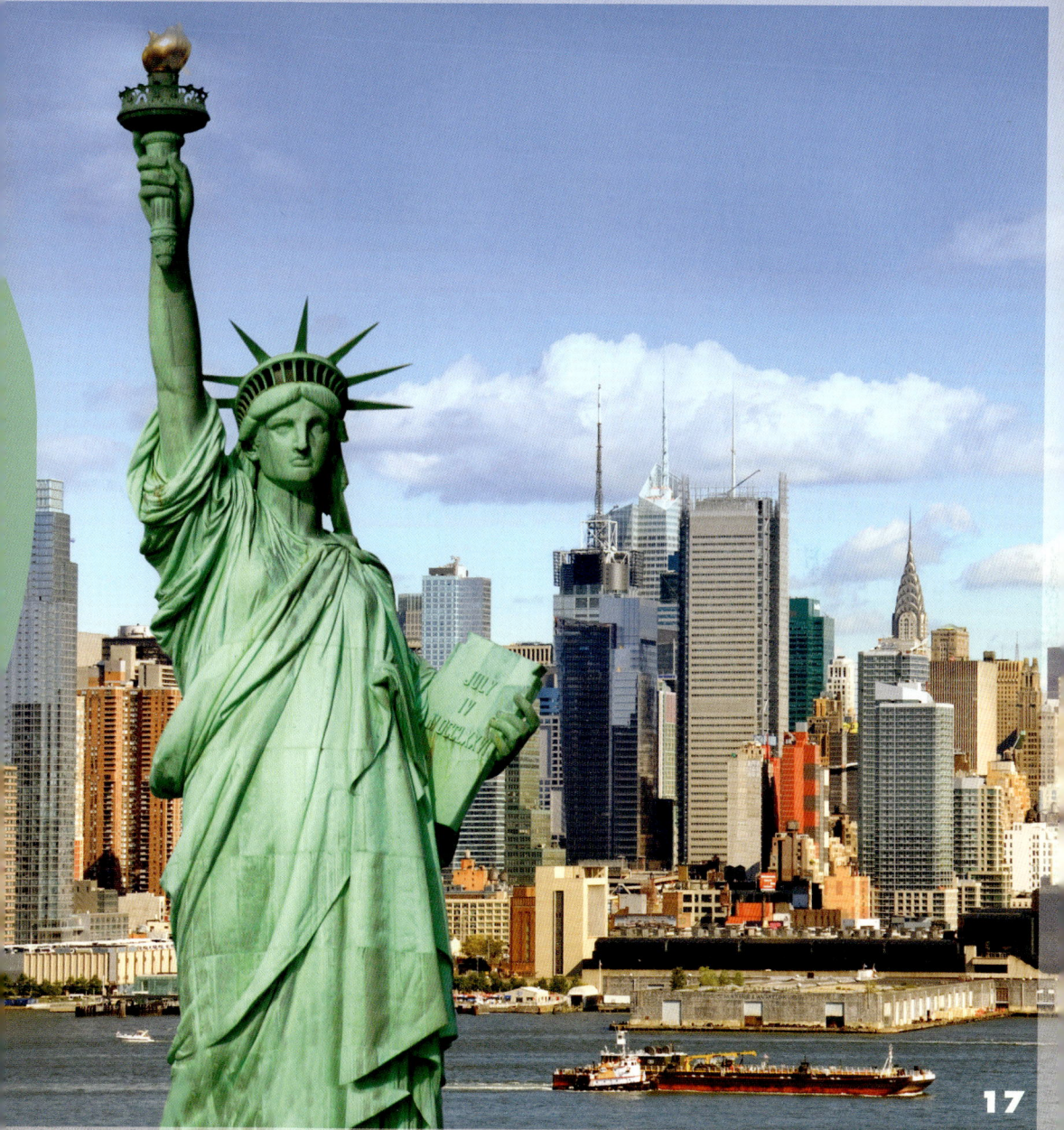

The bus is in front of the
Houses of Parliament.
Can you see Big Ben
behind the bus?
What city is this?

Big Ben

The flag is in front of the city. Can you see the city behind the flag?

What colour is the flag?

Glossary

barn   a farm building used to keep hay and animals in

duckling   a young duck

statue   a person or animal made from stone or metal

Find out more

Eddie and Ellie's Opposites at the Farm, Rebecca Rissman (Raintree, 2013)

Opposites! (Look & Learn), National Geographic Kids (National Geographic Kids, 2012)

Opposites (Board Book), Penny West (Raintree, 2014)

Website

www.bbc.com/bitesize/clips/zy26sbk
This BBC Bitesize video introduces the use of words to describe their location.

Answers to questions

Here are the answers to the questions in the book: Page 6: there are three horses; Page 8: the barn is red; Page 12: there are six pumpkins; Page 14: the dog is black; Page 18: the city is London; Page 20: the flag is red, white and blue.

Comprehension questions

1. Why do the ducklings swim behind their mother?

2. Describe some of the things you might see in a city.

Index